ISBN 978-0-483-59739-6
PIBN 10790707

This book is a reproduction of an important historical work. Forgotten Books uses
state-of-the-art technology to digitally reconstruct the work, preserving the original format
whilst repairing imperfections present in the aged copy. In rare cases, an imperfection in
the original, such as a blemish or missing page, may be replicated in our edition. We do,
however, repair the vast majority of imperfections successfully; any imperfections that
remain are intentionally left to preserve the state of such historical works.

THE GREAT WOR
IN AMERICA

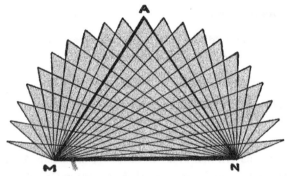

The Philosophy of Individual Life

AUGUST, 1925

Volume I

Number 4

THE GREAT WORK IN AMERICA

A monthly magazine, published by J. E. Richardson, the first day of every month. This journal co-ordinates the known facts and principles of physical Nature with the demonstrated facts and principles of spiritual Nature; giving to the world an authentic statement of the teachings and findings of the Great School Of Natural Science.

Editorial Headquarters, 8186 Marmont Lane, Hollywood, Calif.

EDITORIAL STAFF

Editor-In-Chief . . . . . . J. E. Richardson, TK.

Assistant Editor . . . . . . Noneta S. Richardson

Associate Editors . . . . Joseph A. Sadony
Clarence Thomas and W. W. Mann.

Contributing Editor . . William Alvis Guthrie, M. D.

Senior Grand Lecturer for the U. S. and Director of District No. 8 or the SADOL MOVEMENT

* * * * * * * *

Yearly subscription in U. S. A. $3.25; in Canada $3.50; foreign countries $4.00. Single copies in U. S. A. 35c; in Canada 40c; in foreign countries 50c Back numbers 50c.

Volume I	AUGUST 1925	Number 4

CONTENTS

THE GREAT WOR
IN AMERICA

INSANITY

ITS DIAGNOSIS AND CURE

(CONTINUED)

There are additional manifestations which are of importance in the work of diagnosis of perceptional, or subjective insanity. Every physician of importance has observed them, but, generally speaking, the physician has not understood their significance, and therefore has ignored them entirely. In other words, they have meant nothing to him as aids to correct diagnosis, and he has passed them unnoticed. For this we must not condemn him, for he has but followed the instructions of the school in which he received his education.

1. It often occurs that the case is one of so-called "religious mania". This means that the individual under observation suddenly becomes a religious fanatic. Usually this particular development comes with little or no apparent previous "symptoms" to indicate that it is approaching. The patient may begin to preach, as often occurs. In this event he usually gives himself another name, frequently the name of some evangelist who has passed on to the other side. He is in deadly earnest. He is imbued with the serious business of "saving souls". In many instances his sermons are quite as rational and well constructed as are those of our licensed earthly evangelists. A careful inquiry from him, however, discloses the fact that he is entirely ignorant upon the subject of his sermon. Moreover, he does not know a word of what he has said. He is absolutely unconscious of the thing he has done, as well as of the words he has uttered during his sermons. Hence, the examining physician,

without hesitancy, diagnoses the case as one of "religious mania"—the result of "religious emotionalism".

In at least nine out of every ten cases of this nature, an independent psychic would be able to see, know and identify the spiritual evangelist who has obtained hypnotic control of the patient, and is using him as an automatic instrument through which to get his message over to those upon the physical plane.

In such cases the students and friends of Natural Science may feel themselves justified in diagnosing them as "subjective control"—with the controlling intelligence upon the spiritual plane.

But it must be kept in mind that such cases run the entire scale of symptomatic manifestations. Now and then there is a case of purely physical origin most difficult to differentiate from the class to which I refer. In such exceptions, however, the history of the individual will generally disclose the presence of the physical causes.

And then, a careful study of the case, over a period of two or three days, will show an erratic tendency which, at times, will develop a violence that is inconsistent with a carefully planned line of religious work.

In all such cases a physician (more especially of the naturopathic school) should be given charge of the physical body of the patient, and permitted to use every known physical aid to a restoration of physical health. In most such cases his work will remove the physical cause or disturbance, and the case will recover entirely, even though it may be combined with outside spiritual interferences.

But, if the student and friend will cooperate with the physician, by using such methods as would apply to a case of obsession, he will be of great help and will hasten a perfect cure in every instance.

If the physician is unable to remove the physical disturbance, there is little or no prospect of a cure. On the other hand, intelligent cooperation between physician and psychic diagnostitian will result in rapid recovery.

2. One of the most difficult cases to diagnose correctly is that of outside influence by vicious, licentious, lustful intelli-

gences who seek to gratify an intense and abnormal passion
that has been carried over from this side—due to unrestrained
indulgence of the sex passion while upon the earth plane. Such
degenerate intelligences sink to the lowest rounds of the mag-
netic or mezzanine plane, and are exceedingly slow in overcoming their weakness.

But the chief difficulty in making a correct diagnosis lies
in the fact that the patient, in such cases, is reluctant to admit
that the sexual passion is involved. I have had many cases
where the patient has absolutely and persistently denied that
his sexual appetite and passion were stimulated or intensified
at all; and this when he knew he was a victim of outside spiritual controls, and that the line of direct attack upon him was
that of his physical passions and desires. My own ability to
see and observe and know exactly who the vicious controls
were and the exact nature of their operations were the only
things that enabled me, finally, to obtain a confession of the
truth. False pride is a difficult thing to overcome, and is often
the one thing that stands between such patients and complete
and quick recovery.

In some cases, if the student diagnostitian will convey the
suggestion that he *knows* of the sexual disturbance, he will
obtain an admission with little trouble. Just by a line of questions which carry that suggestion, he will often succeed in
overcoming the false pride of the patient and get the truth.
For instance: "Of course you are having a lot of trouble to
control your sex desires. You need not think anything of this,
for it is almost universal among cases of outside spiritual influences. That is one of their principal lines of attack. You
often actually *feel* the touch of their hands upon your body, do
you not? And then you have to fight with all your might to
keep them from controlling you completely—or compelling you
to go out and seek gratification?" By clever work one may get
the truth without actually having the power to see spiritually.
But this calls for a high degree of intelligence and cleverness,
in gaining the confidence of the patient.

3. There are also many cases of spiritual influences where
the line of attack is the appetite for liquor, or drugs. In the
very largest number of cases of "periodical drunkenness", or

uncontrollable spasms of desire for liquor, the entire cause is that of a low order of spiritual intelligences who have indulged their appetites for liquor, or drugs, upon the earth plane, until they became helpless victims of the habit. These carry their habit and appetite over, at physical death, and use every opportunity to find a victim they can control through whom to obtain such gratification as they can from the spiritual side of life. Few upon the physical plane have any idea of the vast army of spiritual people who have to be educated by the Borderland Workers until they overcome the destructive appetites and desires they have carried over at death.

But, if the students and friends who know of these conditions, will but make use of their intelligence wisely, they will be able to get the truth from almost every patient, in due time and by the exercise of the utmost patience and forbearance.

This covers the subject of diagnosis, as far as seems advisable at present. There are many phases of the subject which I have not even suggested. But I feel that they should be reserved for a much fuller and more detailed consideration, later on. It has been my hope and intention to add a volume, upon the general subject, to the Harmonic Series.

In my next article I desire to take up the subject of the methods of treatment and cure of all forms of subjective insanity, and I hope I shall be able to give to my readers valuable information that will enable them to become my Helpers in the work of passing on the knowledge of the Great School where it will accomplish the largest measure of good to humanity in the years to come. (To be continued.)

J. E. RICHARDSON, TK.

4

From the Valley of the Pines.

PINE NEEDLES
JOSEPH A. SADONY

ASPIRATION.
A beautiful green meadow covers the unsightly earth of dead resolutions.

Each blade of grass is a monument to the masses.

Each flower reaching into the air is a monument to the genius, the martyr, the man or the woman who dares carry out the aspiration of their souls.

REALIZATION.
Be happy in the thought that all your possibilities and blessings thus far have not unfolded themselves.

You still have before you a realization beyond your present comprehension.

It is impossible for you to draw a picture which you have not seen unless you make it a composite, using that which is already in memory.

But it requires new actual experiences, and new emotions and new designs which you acquire from environments, to make you realize greater sensations and joys.

UNDERSTANDING.
You know we often think ourselves misunderstood, when it is we ourselves who misunderstand others.

THE BORDERLINE OF PAIN AND SORROW
It is best that we live on the borderline of pain and sorrow that we may the better realize our duty and our mission. And that we may be constantly awake to danger.

We must ever avoid too much pain, or we shall become calloused and heedless of the warning when the limitations of one of Nature's laws has been reached.

Indeed, that is what pain is, such a waning.

Daily contact with an enemy results in the enemy being despised.

But if he is avoided, he creates another weapon to hurt in his absence.

The farther removed the more horrible the cry of the battle-field. . . . .

Problems and misfortunes are blessings of immunity to oblivion and failure. They awaken and exercise a sluggish brain. They strengthen faith and hope born in the Soul.

But if sorrows and calamities go by unnoticed,—if no lesson has been learned, then a life has been in vain.

How can we enjoy without having known sorrow?

How can we know sorrow without joy?

Sympathy is born in sorrow.

Appreciation often dies in joy.

But the memory of both sorrow and joy awakens faith, hope and charity, consideration, kindness and love.

TODAY.

I believe that if we wish to go to the attic rooms of a house, we must first pass through the door of the lower floor.

Men are not endowed with the legs of a grasshopper.

We are supposed to take one step at a time. . . .

And then, too, we can hardly speak with exactness of the Infinite, Incomprehensible, Omnipotence, when viewed from our place on the top of a toad-stool.

There is enough here before us for several life-times for analysis.

Why should we waste our time inventing new names for "Bread", when it is becoming moldy before we have taken the first bite? . . . .

Life is too short to try and call out and memorize the stations from earth to heaven. It is far easier and less confusing to call them out as we pass through them on our way toward heaven.

Let us watch the stew upon the stove.

Or the pudding in the oven . . . today.

And not worry about the untried recipe which is still in the "Abstract".

6

CROSSES.

The man who really carries a burden finds no time to brag or complain about it.

There are many who smile and carry heavy crosses.

But the heaviest cross here is like the cross of a certain man who complained.

He daily complained of the heavy cross that he was forced to carry.

Until one night he dreamed a dream.

He dreamed that he was dead.

He dreamed that when he reached heaven, the gentle hand of the Master Jesus led him to a large field where thousands and thousands of crosses were strewn upon the ground.

Some were large, some small.

Wide, narrow, heavy, light crosses!

And all were made from One Cross!

Jesus said, "Choose, my son, the cross you wish to carry, for I have divided my little cross with all the world."

So the man searched, and at last he found the smallest cross of all.

He placed it upon his shoulder and started homeward.

When he reached home, he awoke, and found that he had chosen his Own Cross,—the Cross of which he had complained so bitterly.

CONTENTMENT.

When a man is entirely worldly contented, he is simply dead to the world as far as others are concerned.

A man who is so entirely contented has no object to strive for.

But a man can never be entirely thus contented as long as there are things that he wants, or that are out of the reach of his ambition.

Have you known what desire means?

I always feel that if I am contented, I am through with that particular aspiration with which I have been striving. . . . .

If a man desires to be wealthy, he strives day and night until old age creeps upon him,

And at last he acquires his wealth.

His desires and ambitions are now ended.

He does not desire to be what he already is.

He is contented and is a part of what he has created.

But another man who truly loves a woman!

His desire and ambition are to possess her love.

He succeeds.

Does his desire wane in the knowledge that he possesses it?

It will never end!

Still he is contented, but will never have enough of this true love as long as he lives.

It is this contentment which speaks of eternity.

The common contentment of the world can be swept away in a moment,

But contentment from true love, never!

Try to awaken the true love that is hidden deep in your heart.

WANTS.

Most men die from want of a want.

A man without a want or set purpose, depending upon the intensity of his personality, is bound to let the reins slip.

The banker who retires has no want.

The educator who is through with the exercises of his executive ability has no want.

He shortly dies.

The lover has perhaps the greatest material want.

You can readily see the energy and endurance involved!

The hermit has a subtle want, and with all hardships, lives to a ripe old age.

The philosopher has an eternal want and so lives on forever, for by his knowledge he has outstripped death. And when he passes death's portals his words of wisdom and deeds of kindness live on. . . . .

A want is valued by the effort made.

The effort made denotes the quality and the quantity of its consummation.

We all have whims. We entertain false desires,—-picked up, perhaps, from the broadcasting of those we meet.

Often we have an appetite for a certain food, which proves nauseating when placed before us.

Whence came the appetite?

8

It behooves us to be sure that we want what we think we want, for when the want is once satisfied, we must use it rightly that it may prove a blessing and not a curse.

It is meant that we should always have a want.

Without it our mental energy refuses to work. It is as the photographic plate refuses to record without the irritation of light.

If music hath charms, does not the sound find reflection in the emotions of the heart?

Are not all living creatures but halves of a complete whole?

This law may be seen operating throughout nature . . . the halves differing only in degree or polarity.

Destroying want hinders Nature's aim and design to create a complete unit through an evolution toward perfection.

MYSTERY AND PSYCHISM.

You have told me that you take an hour each day for silence and prayer. This will surely help you find yourself.

Seek seclusion if you wish to become acquainted with yourself. But try to add one kind deed to each hour of prayer.

Make someone happy!

It will surprise you what benefit you will derive.

For no kind act is ever lost under the law of compensation.

There is much to look forward to. But be very careful of those who profess to be spiritually inclined and claim to teach you spiritual things, unless they can show you examples, and live in their homes as they profess.

To consider a man carefully, never look on his front porch, but go into the alley in the rear of his house.

Inspiration of truth is as free as the air, as bright as the sun, and as pure as the clearest dew.

The three most essential elements of life are sunshine, air and water.

And you will find pure air odorless, pure water tasteless, and loving deeds priceless.

If you are engaged in a "study" of psychism, I would advise you to proceed very slowly and carefully. Make no mistake, for it is very dangerous.

9

Let me assure you that I am in a position to know.

I understand "circles".

And I warn you as a friend and a brother, "Be cautious".

It is in dealing with that which may cause you to lose your individuality, that you need fear for your freedom and your happiness.

It is unwise to try to run before you are able to creep, and as well, dangerous.

So I warn you not to be engrossed in such researches.

For those things worth while are very scarce, and yet so simple to understand.

Remember all those things which are permanent, each has an individuality of its own.

So you must eat nothing that is not appetizing, easy to digest and wholesome.

For when you feed your brain, you either awaken the Soul, or you lull it to sleep.

Ever bear in mind to stay away from things of mystery.

God works and labors in the light alone.

Avoïd superstition, for that extinguishes the light of truth.

Go slowly, a step at a time, and as soon as you get weary, you will find new strength.

Remember always, that one must pay a penny for a penny's worth of bread.

By all means refrain from going to "mediums", or you will become confused, and perhaps deceïved.

To become a "medium" is to be cast upon a new earth of mystery and phantoms. To behold wonderful things, and yet be no wiser. To be a stranger, with an unknown tongue.

The work of spiritual unfoldment cannot be taught in one year. It requires a life-time.

And you will not be given the key of knowledge until you will not desecrate the room within. . . . .

Again, it is not enough that we travel in the forest of Knowledge.

We must blaze our trail so that we can return home safely.

And let me add:

He who barters the fruits of wisdom destroys the seed of understanding.

A philosopher will clothe his knowledge with the cloth of understanding so that a worthy eye can discern its symbols, and without price.

EDITOR'S NOTES:

"Destroying want hinders Nature's aim and design to create a complete unit through an evolution to perfection."

This sentence expresses, if uniquely, one of the great operative principles so fully treated in the Harmonic Series of the teaching of the Great School. Mr. Sadony has touched the subject of Want or Desire, in his own personal way. And yet I think the following may show how completely his words are in accord with the findings of Natural Science.

Surely, to be without a want is to merely exist. It is not to live in a specific sense of the word. A natural active demand of the Soul is for satisfaction, for realization. And Want or Desire is that active demand. It is expressed very definitely in The Great Work. Desire "represents the Soul's fundamental search for satisfaction. It is based upon the Soul's primary and inherent craving for realization."

It follows that as Want or Desire is a primary activity or craving of the Soul, it is most necessary that man as an intelligent being should give attention to his wants.

In the first place, he should see to it that he has wants. It is perfectly natural to want food. There is seldom a lack of that demand. But there are other wants of his spiritual and psychical natures, which as urgently cry out for satisfaction. These are both for preservation of life and for the development of the individual.

Should other wants fail, there is one want that seems ever present, and that is man's desire to live. Even though suffering pain and enduring starvation, man will cling as long as possible to life in the body.

Man does really want to live and to live fully.

Then he should see to his wants. For it is only by the stinging stimulus of wants that he will grow in the various elements of his nature. It is only by wants that the Soul is

11

brought into cognizable relationships with the various departments of Nature, physical, spiritual and psychical.

It is basically by wants that the Soul receives sensations, experience and finally knowledge. It is by wants that the Consciousness is enabled to expand, and the desirous element of the Soul becomes a part of it.

It is stated in The Great Work, "In its specific and determinate sense Desire is but a mode of Consciousness."

It then appears that Desire or Want is a necessary mode of Consciousness to preserve intelligent individualized life. It is really a phase of Consciousness necessary to really live and to experience life fully, and to gain knowledge. For Desire is at the roots of hope and faith. And—"Faith is a perpetual inspiration" for the acquisition of sensation, experience and knowledge.

It is also then clear that in the way of Spiritual Growth and Unfoldment the Want and Desire play important parts. "Every demand of the Soul for satisfaction along certain specific lines becomes a conscious sensation. . . . And the Soul experiences the sense of craving or desire in all departments of individual being."

It must appear from the foregoing, if we reason correctly, that this primary craving of the Soul for realization, this wanting and desiring becomes the means by which man is able consciously to fit himself with advantage into the evolutionary scheme of Nature. It seems that he might knowingly assist Nature in evolving a man who not only has the use of his world consciousness, but who might develop a cosmic consciousness. Quoting from The Great Work, "The process of Spiritual Development is but the process of enlarging the scope and expanding the limitations of individual consciousness."

The expressed goal of so many philosophies, and contemplative and mystical exercises is this desired state of Cosmic, or Enlarged Consciousness. Much has been written on the subject. And a considerable number of men throughout the ages have been noted as having attained such a state of Consciousness. Yet there have always been danger signals posted for the wayfarer, warning him against desires. Some philosophies have stressed the necessity of "killing out" all desire, if Spiritual Unfoldment is to be attained. Religious writings abound with the injunction to those who strive for a realization of the spiritual life, that they should erase from consciousness all inordinate cravings. They impress the reader that the mind should be without images and free of desires. It has been taught by some religions that even intense desire for spiritual advancement defeats the purpose of the aspirant.

But the wiser have usually followed such instructions with the admonition also to beware of "Passivity". There is a "rest" in Nature greatly to be desired. But there is an activity in rest, that is a Soul exercise which brings about a closer union with the harmonics of Nature.

The perfect way of Spiritual Unfoldment is traversed by the exercise of a piercing love, an inward longing, and an insatiable hunger which seek satisfaction in harmony with all Nature.

Emptying himself of this longing, depriving himself of the use of the love force, emptying himself of desire, man attains a false contentment, an egotistical pride, and self-complacency which carry him along the "broad highway".

If man had not the power of Free-Will, and if he had not the capacity of making a choice of his Wants and Desires, then indeed would those who cry "kill desire" have sufficient reason for their injunction. But here, as in so many other things, it is the misuse of Wants and Desires that retards man's growth, and brings future penalties. It is his misuse of powers, capacities, and attributes which brings forth the destructive element in man's life.

The whole matter resolves itself into what Wants and Desires will man admit to Consciousness, and in what degree. It is plainly seen that if all wants were freely admitted to Consciousness, man would have no intelligent part in making himself the master of his destiny.

But man can have an intelligent part in assisting Nature in her plan if he so wills.

Man has been endowed with a Will, and the intelligent power to choose what Desires and Wants he will entertain. It is then incumbent upon him so to exercise this Will, to hold it

13

forever and always free, and indeed be ruler over the Kingdom of his Soul.

Man should set up within this kingdom, his Free-Will as his Prime Minister. This Minister should be entrenched and made safe in his citadel of Chosen Wants and Desires. In his right hand he should hold a staff of strength and might, that the choice of man's wants shall receive satisfaction and realization. In his left hand he should hold a transparent light of morality, which will bring the Wants and Desires into harmony with intelligence and reason. Thus will the Prime Minister keep order and cleanliness in the kingdom of man's Soul. And thus will the man attain virtue, be in concord with Nature's harmonic laws, expand his Consciousness, and experience Spiritual Unfoldment.

Man as an intelligent individual is engrossed in a particular struggle for Self-Completion. All his Wants and Desires are admitted into his Consciousness with such a hope and faith. And this brings us back to the quotation at the beginning of this note. "Destroying want hinders Nature's aim and design to create a complete unit through an evolution to perfection."

A quotation from the Harmonics of Evolution will add emphasis. "A man desires, wills and universally attempts to execute his individual desires and designs. This innate power of individual will constitutes the motor power in the self-evolution of intelligent beings."

It must not be overlooked that Nature in an universal way is also engaged in the plan to develop a complete individual. Her one great principle operating toward that end is universal and fundamental.

And at the roots of all Wants and Desires in man, is that fundamental principle of Nature "which impels every entity to seek vibratory correspondence with another like entity of opposite polarity". That is the search for satisfaction, realization, happiness and harmony.

Brought down to a final analysis, all Wants and Desires are cravings of the Soul for its own satisfaction, realization, happiness and harmony. And each man is the master of his own Soul. He can build his happiness, or he can destroy it. This is his personal search. He can assist Nature in her great plan, or he can hinder. This is his responsibility. He can accelerate his development toward Self-Completion, or he can retard it. It all depends upon how he conforms his Wants and Desires, and the execution of them, to spiritual principles, and to the constructive evolutionary process of Nature.

CLARENCE THOMAS.

THE LAKE OF BEAUTY

Let your mind be quiet, realizing the beauty of the world, and the immense, the boundless treasures that it holds in store.

All that you have within you, all that your heart desires, all that your Nature so specially fits you for—that or the counterpart of it waits embedded in the great Whole, for you. It will surely come to you.

Yet equally surely not one moment before its appointed time will it come. All your crying and fever and reaching out of hands will make no difference.

Therefore, do not begin that game at all.

Do not recklessly spill the waters of your mind in this direction and in that, lest you become like a spring lost and dissipated in the desert.

But draw together into a little compass, and hold them still, so still;

And let them become clear, so clear—so limpid, so mirror-like;

At last the mountains and the sky shall glass themselves in peaceful beauty,

And the antelope shall descend to drink, and to gaze at his reflected image, and the lion to quench his thirst,

And Love himself shall come and bend over, and catch his own likeness in you.

—*From "Toward Democracy," by Edward Carpenter.*

15

INDIVIDUALITY

"Being a parent seems the simplest and most natural thing in the world—to those who have never tried it. But to one who has looked down in awe and wonder upon that small mass of protoplasm and soul that we call a babe, it is different. To him who has seen in some wee ape the replica of himself, parenthood is a serious business. To be responsible for that new life from downy poll to pink toe-nails. To have brought out of nothingness this poor little mortal to try issues with the great world! To see a pitifully helpless organism of our creation made the home of a living soul whose value we may not know and whose destiny we cannot conceive—is not all this enough to give one pause?"—(Geo. H. Betts.)

With the birth of the child its postnatal education begins. If the mother has fulfilled her parental responsibility the foundation of this education has been established during the period of gestation, for the postnatal education is but a continuation of the prenatal. The individual soul has taken possession of the physical body provided by Nature and the mother, and is about to take up its life on the physical plane. It is prepared and equipped now to continue its work of unfoldment and development through education and the acquisition of knowledge through experience on the earth plane. It is about to undertake its work of Self-Completion, that is, the development of itself equally physically, spiritually and psychically.

The mother has assumed the responsibility of assisting the child in its development and unfoldment, until such time as it is able to know the "Right Way from the Wrong" and to follow its own road to successful manhood or womanhood.

Because of the close relationship existing between the mother and the child during the prenatal period, and her influence and control over it, the mother necessarily is closest to, and exerts greatest influence over, her child (immediately after birth, and until it is old enough to be influenced by other external conditions) of any person. The consciousness of the child is accustomed to the mother's influence and association. It looks to the mother for sustenance and protection and help. It depends upon the mother for life, as well as for leadership. The facts make it self-evident, therefore, that the mother has paramount influence over the education of her child postnatally, and that she is the greatest living factor in its postnatal education. She holds within her power the postnatal life and education of the soul she has helped to bring into the world.

The mother's *postnatal* responsibility begins with the *birth* of the child, and is a continuation of her *prenatal* responsibility. Her postnatal influence and education must, therefore, be a continuation of her prenatal control. In order that she may fulfill this responsibility successfully, it is important that she undertake the education of her child immediately from the moment of its birth. This means that she must have been previously educated herself, and prepared, prior to pregnancy, to undertake her postnatal responsibility. This points out the importance of the mother's self-education; for one cannot impart knowledge unless one possesses knowledge to impart.

Again, we have the mother's two-fold responsibility, namely, to educate herself, and to educate her child.

The following articles to appear deal only with the moral phase of the mother's responsibility to all her children—but more especially to her daughters. They are intended as a course of study in practical psychology for mothers. They represent a code of ethics and morality for the education of mothers, as well as that of their children. They are given in an endeavor to help the mothers of today realize their responsibility, in a moral sense, to their children, and to inspire them to discharge that responsibility, in order that they may merit just guerdon, under the Law of Compensation, for obligations fulfilled and responsibilities discharged. It is hoped they may prove an inspiration to mothers, and help them to make of this generation of womanhood the greatest in history.

The first subject under consideration is that of *Individuality*. It is a subject of vital importance to the life and development of every individual; yet no other subject is so generally misunderstood, misinterpreted, overlooked and ignored by the large majority of people. True, it is a much mooted question among students of psychology; yet, in the essential meaning

17

and practical application, it proves to be one of the most intangible and elusive subjects to the students themselves and to the average man or woman of society in general.

What *is* Individuality?

Individuality is the general expression of the inherent characteristics of the individual soul, at any given time, which characteristics differentiate it from every other living soul.

The Declaration of Independence states that *"all men are created equal"*. But are they? If so, why are some born idiots, while others come into the world equipped with splendid intelligences and the abilities to use them? Why do some enter earth life with beautiful, lofty and ennobled souls, while others come with blackened souls weighted down with crime, dishonesty and immorality? Why are some born into the infant, Negro race, while others come into the maturer white race? *Why* are these things true? We know they are; but *why?*

In one sense, the statement that all men are *"created"* equal, is true. That is to say, all men, all individual *souls,* are created with certain similar and equal equipment—inalienable rights, privileges and prerogatives, and a definite purpose. Each soul, as it is created, is equipped with a consciousness, a Will, and a full set of capacities, faculties and powers, as well as appetites, passions, emotions, desires, ambitions and aspirations. These are Nature's gifts to him, and to every other human soul. Therefore, in general equipment men are "created equal".

Again, every individual soul is provided by Nature with certain inalienable rights, privileges and prerogatives—which are "Life, Liberty and the Pursuit of Individual Happiness". These constitute the rights of every human being at the time of "creation". Therefore, all men are created equal—in their inalienable rights.

Again, every soul is created by Nature, with a definite purpose—that of Self-Completion. Therefore, all men are created with an equal purpose.

We will agree, therefore, that all men are *created* equal, in equipment, inalienable rights and purpose. We admit this. Nevertheless, in spite of this similarity and equality, we must admit further, from personal observation and experience, that men are *born into this physical life* essentially different from one another. Note the fact carefully that a careful differentiation is made between the *"creation"* of a soul, and the event of its "birth into this physical life".

Has any person ever known two people absolutely alike in essential character? Have you, kind reader? No. You may have met types, or certain people who apparently were alike in generalities. But always, upon close study and careful analysis, inevitably you find them essentially different in the deeper things of life. Then, wherein lies this essential difference? There is but one answer—it lies in INDIVIDUALITY.

Nature's great, essential and underlying plan and purpose would seem to be the individualizing of intelligence. From the very lowest form of animal life to the very highest of the human we see traces of this plan being worked out. All scientific study, analysis, observation and experience, in the final summing up, lead to the definite conclusion that the individualizing and developing of intelligence are the great aim and purpose of God, or Nature, or the Great Creator. All the sophistry and specious reasoning ever invented have been unable to find any other purpose of Nature—with reference to individual life. All evidence bears out this fact of Nature's great plan and purpose.

In the execution of her general plan—the individualizing of intelligence—Nature seems to have a definite scheme, or method, for differentiating each intelligence from every other. Each is given an individual mark, or "brand", as a distinguishing feature. In each she makes a fundamental, underlying and essential difference, which differentiates that soul from all other entities of its kind. In each she imparts certain idiocyncrasies, eccentricities, merits and demerits, likes and dislikes. Some have greater "intelligence *to know*", others greater "courage *to dare*", still others greater "perseverance *to do*". But after the creation of each individual intelligence, Nature "breaks the mould", as it were, so there never is or can be but one of a kind. In other words, she implants in each and every human soul *Individuality*.

It is evident that, on the physical plane, Nature uses *personality* as her distinguishing mark or "brand", of physical

19

organisms. For, never were two physical organisms exactly alike, even though belonging to the same species. Each has its peculiar personality. As this is true on the physical plane, so it seems to be a fixed part of Nature's great plan and purpose to use *Individuality* as her distinguishing mark, or "badge", on the *Soul* plane. She creates no two souls exactly alike. Each has its differentiating *Individuality*. This she does to protect her individualizing process.

The scheme of *Individuality* is illustrated in the fact that no two oak trees have ever been known to be exactly alike. While the acorns from which these trees develop may have been seemingly alike, in general pattern and formation; yet, in essential form and in the potentialities which they embodied, they were very unlike. If not, then the trees necessarily must hav been exactly alike in size, shape, height, conformation, etc.

The same is equally true of two crystals. The outward form and appearance may seem to be alike, yet they are essentially different, nevertheless; for the individuality is ever present, and never can be overcome. Nature has established individuality as her distinguishing mark *in the kingdom of the soul.*

All that has been suggested by the foregoing, and vastly more which might be suggested, only serve to show the importance which Nature attaches to *individuality,* and the vital relation it bears to the great underlying purpose of individual life.

The question of the essential difference in human beings has been mooted among the greatest scientists and philosophers of all ages. Many explanations and analyses are given, all of which are intensely fascinating—to anyone interested in the subject.

The ancient Hindu philosophy of life endeavors to account for this difference, and claims to answer the question in the doctrine of *"Reincarnation".* By Reincarnation is meant the repeated return of the same human soul in different human forms—physical *bodies.* It holds that a soul is *"created" only once,* but that it may be *"born into physical life" many times.*

For instance, one human soul, let us say, has lived on the physical plane and has inhabited five different physical bodies. Each time it has lived on this plane, the soul has acquired knowledge, through experience, peculiar to the conditions and environment in which it was born. At the end of its fifth incarnation, it has acquired an enormous stock of valuable knowledge and experience.

Another human soul has returned to earth life, let us say, but twice. In that time it has required knowledge incident to its conditions and environment, but necessarily has gained less experience because of the limit of time and opportunity.

Both souls return to the earth at the same time—in yet *another* reincarnation. From birth, the older soul manifests great wisdom, intelligence, knowledge, etc. While their physical bodies are of the same age, yet it is evident that the *souls* inhabiting these different bodies are ages apart, in point of development. This, the ancient Hindus claim, is due to the greater number of incarnations of the one soul, and therefore, its infinitely greater knowledge gained through experience in its various earth lives. Thus they solve the question of inequality and difference in human beings.

Other Orientals account for this essential difference in the doctrine of "transmigration of souls", by which they mean the transit of human souls through the lower forms of animal life. Still others solve the problem—to their own apparent satisfaction—through their belief in the Law of Compensation.

A large part of the Occident, however, seems to lean most to the doctrine of "Special Creation." This doctrine holds that each soul is actually *"created"* at physical birth. In other words, that each time a child is born into the physical world, a new soul is "created".

This often brings up the question of just how the votaries of this doctrine account for the fact that some souls almost at physical birth begin to show that they possess unusual knowledge and intelligence; while others seem never to possess these, during their entire physical existence.

Many theories are propounded, by various cults and religions throughout the world, concerning this subject of differentiation in individuals. Nevertheless, all people recognize the existence of *Individuality* as a fundamental principle in Nature. They vary only in accounting for the cause or reason back of it.

Individuality is a fact in Nature. It is an undeniable fact. It is a fact all people recognize and accept. It is a fact upon

21

which Nature places great importance. It causes each individual soul to seek its own path, its own interests, its own lines of endeavor, its own methods of procedure, to gain its own goal, and to merit its own reward. Because of it, every individual must think for himself, and judge his own thoughts, actions and motives. No other person can do it for him. And, because of it, every human being is a sentient, immortal soul who must live his *own* life, die his *own* death, and be accountable to the Giver of all Life, for his *own* deeds and development and destiny, under the Great Law of Compensation.

Since Individuality, then, is such a vital and an essential fact in Nature, what moral right has any individual to ignore, disregard, suppress, or endeavor to eliminate it? What can an individual ever gain by living in ignorance of his own individuality, or by being intolerant with that of others? And what shall be his penalty for violation of the law?

The fact that Individuality is essential and fundamental, as an underlying principle in Nature, should awaken every human being to a sense of his individual responsibility to recognize it, study it, apply it, respect it, honor it, and conform to the law which governs it. This is his fixed duty and obligation.

Likewise, this is the duty and obligation of every *mother*. She must educate herself in the subject of *Individuality;* she must study it; she must realize its importance in regard to the development of life. She must recognize it in herself, and in her children; she must be tolerant with, and generous toward, it in other people; and she must conform to the law which governs its application to herself and to all others.

If the mother finds a vast difference in the individuality of her children, her duty is, not to be disappointed, resentful and heart-broken, but to study each child as an *individual,* and strive to develop the constructive characteristics of *each,* according to its own needs. She must study the idiocyncrasies, merits and demerits, likes and dislikes of each, encourage their separate and distinct constructive penchants, and use every legitimate and available means to encourage the expression of the inherent individuality of each soul and intelligently guide it along *constructive lines*.

A large percentage of the mothers of this age look upon

their children, to some extent, as a burden, or as an encumbrance to be accepted as a necessary part of life. They accept them as a matter of course, but as a thing to be shunted as much as possible, so as not to interfere with the even tenor of their own lives.

The average mother is so selfishly engrossed in her own life and interests that her children and their higher interests are, to her, but secondary. Her general attitude seems to be to rear them, yes, but with as little effort and care on her part as possible. She knows little concerning the subject of individuality, and cares less. The individuality of her children is of little or no importance or interest to her; a study of it is out of the question, for that involves time and effort on her part and interferes with her own personal and selfish interests. Their individual penchants—so far as she is concerned—are of little consequence to anyone but themselves; so, why should she trouble to encourage them? Their interests lie entirely outside the field of her own; why should she endeavor to educate herself in those lines?

And so the average mother endeavors to rear her children, provide food, clothing, shelter, and school education for them, and perhaps to pay a teacher to instruct them in music and dancing. Beyond this point, however, the children are shunted and ignored and thrown upon their own resources or those of outsiders.

Again: Some of our "modern" mothers who are so engrossed in themselves and in their own interests that they fail in their responsibilities to their children, excuse themselves on this score: "My children, Mary and Johnny, both have such strong and decided individualities that I am just allowing them to go their own ways, and do just as they please. In this way they will fully develop their individualities without interference. And I believe in Individuality."

And so do I. But I say this mother is failing quite as grossly in her responsibility as is the mother who ignores Individuality. For Individuality must have intelligent *guidance* as well as recognition—otherwise it becomes over-exaggerated, develops an enlarged egotism and is destructive in all of its tendencies.

23

Suppose a mother has three daughters. The eldest shows a marked leaning toward music. The middle one reveals a deep spiritual nature; while the attention of the youngest is directed toward athletics. How would the average mother deal with these diversified individualities? How would she meet her problem?

Let us say, for the sake of illustration, that the mother's penchant is for dancing—a line separate and distinct from those of her three daughters. The mother realizes, in a vague sort of way, that her children are interested in lines which hold no interest for her. She is disappointed and resentful because of this, and because, as she thinks, she can find no companionship with them. She recognizes no *individuality* and respects no penchant. She has no interest in music, athletics or spiritual things, and makes no effort to educate herself in any of these lines.

The eldest daughter comes to the mother to counsel her concerning music. She finds the mother uneducated in this line of endeavor, and devoid of interest. She finds her indifferent and unresponsive. She is conscious of an undercurrent of intolerance and resentment in the mother.

The second daughter goes to the mother to question her concerning things spiritual. In an intolerant sort of way she is shunted, perhaps with some sort of polite excuse. She receives not the slightest suggestion of sympathy, of understanding, or of kind response. She leaves, impressed with the intangible feeling of antagonism on the part of the mother.

The athletic daughter endeavors to interest her mother in gymnastics, tennis, baseball, or other athletics of interest to her. She finds the mother ignorant of these things, lacking in interest, unresponsive and indifferent. She leaves her, disheartened, and conscious of an essential deficiency on the part of the mother.

This lack of general education, interest, responsiveness, tolerance, generosity and sympathy, only serves to close the door of confidence, understanding, mutual fellowship and active companionship between the mother and her daughter. It erects a barrier between them which may never be removed. It acts as an obstruction to the development of the individual penchant

24

of each daughter. It drives them all out of the home, to seek, among other people, for sympathy, interest and companionship in their several lines of endeavor. Most lamentable of all, this tends to suppress their individuality, and necessarily to hamper their soul growth. By virtue of these undesirable results, the mother has failed in her two-fold responsibility—to herself and to her daughters.

How different is this from the sagacious, prudent and intelligent mother who knows her responsibility and endeavors to discharge it, who has educated herself to understand her children, and who rejoices at their marked individualities. She studies each as a separate and distinct unit of intelligence. She learns the eccentricities peculiar to each. She holds herself interested in the three lines of their endeavor by constantly educating herself along these several lines. She encourages each in the development of her individuality, all the while guiding her intelligently in her unfoldment and guarding her against Selfishness and an exalted Ego.

Cleverly and wisely she encourages each daughter to express herself in her own peculiar penchant. She discusses music with her eldest daughter; listens attentively to her chats, and enjoys the demonstrations of her ability, provides every possible opportunity for her progress in that line; attends concerts and musical occasions with her; and keeps her provided with current literature and materials appropriate to that field of work. If she cannot afford to buy these, she obtains them from the libraries. She educates *herself* in music—to the extent that she may be able to sympathize, understand and respond to the needs of her daughter, and be a companion to her in her particular line of interest. This does not mean that she herself needs become an artist in music. By manifesting a wholesome interest in her daughter's work, she quietly and unassumingly encourages her in her penchant, and establishes the daughter's confidence in her as a chum and guide.

Toward her middle daughter she reveals the same interest in the field of her mental leaning. She quietly and sagaciously encourages the child by opening discussions, asking questions, attending lectures, or studying philosophy with her. She educates herself in religions and philosophies—to the extent that

25

she may travel side by side with her daughter who is especially interested in these things. If the religious ideas of her child differ from her own, she bears in mind that the child is an individual entitled to her own ideas; and she maintains a generous attitude and respects her ideas. If she believes her child is wrong in her reasonings, she does not antagonize her, but by persuasive and logical discussions gradually appeals to her reason and tactfully leads her to the right way.

She gains the love, respect and confidence of her youngest daughter by joining her in her athletics; keeps herself apprised of current events in this field; attends exhibition games with her, and always responds to her whenever the child seeks help, advice or companionship. She keeps herself sufficiently educated in this line, so that she may be able at all times to give intelligent companionship to her daughter in any line pertinent to the general field of athletics.

To each daughter, and her respective penchant, the mother is always a responsive listener, an interested associate, an appreciative chum, an active helper, an assiduous coworker, an intelligent guide and a beautiful ideal. Toward each she manifests kindness, tolerance, generosity, unselfish sympathy, active interest and abiding love. In each she inspires charity, forbearance, respect, self-reliance, broad sympathy, sisterly love and an appreciation of wholesome education. Over each she exercises restraint only in those characteristics and tendencies which are abnormal or destructive to soul growth.

This mother, in her wisdom and intelligence, performs her duty, fulfils her obligation and discharges her two-fold responsibility—to herself as an individual intelligence, and to her three daughters, as sentient, immortal individualities. Toward her sons this mother maintains the same interested, helpful and constructive Attitude of Soul.

Let each mother, then, begin at once to recognize the Individuality of the Soul which is in her charge. Let her encourage the unfoldment of that Individuality, assist in the development of it and guide it intelligently along constructive ways, that it may be unselfish always and tolerant of the principle of Individuality in others.

"There is a realm of spiritual parenthood, the realm of

26

sympathy, comradeship and understanding. It is by entering fully into this realm that we become parents *to* our children. When physical parenthood has been completed, spiritual parenthood is just beginning. The process of physical parenthood ends with the birth of the child; the relationships of spiritual parenthood end only with life itself."—(Betts.)

"No one can live another's life, nor solve another's problems; the Divine purpose, which has made us individuals, forces each to do that for himself. But the mother may greatly help —or she may hinder."—(Mrs. H. J. Hersey.)

NONETA S. RICHARDSON.

Flower in the crannied wall,
I pluck you out of the crannies;
I hold you here, root and all, in my hand,
Little flower—but *if* I could understand
What you are, root and all, and all in all,
I should know what God and man is.

—Alfred Tennyson.

"AS ABOVE, SO BELOW"
By J. W. NORWOOD

This aphorism is one of ancient wisdom with which we are more familiar in the Jewish version, "God created man in His own image." It sums up what wise men in all ages have observed of the operation of the one great law—Vibration. It is the same throughout Nature.

The Atom is a miniature solar system.

The cell is patterned after the atom.

The human physical body is patterned after the cell.

Man's spiritual body is patterned after the physical.

Man himself is the highest development of intelligence by virtue of his spirituality.

Intelligence comes from "Above"—that is from Superconsciousness.

And it returns to "Above" after passing through the Selfizing process which constitutes all that we know of physical existence.

It leaves above as universal energy and returns below as selfized energy.

Here on this earth we are concerned daily with the life in which we live far more than in the life we expect to live hereafter.

It may indeed be as we have been told for ages, that there are other cycles of life above this—many of them—which are lived in other worlds and on other planes of existence. If so—and there is no reason for any student to doubt it—it is unquestionably true that the manner in which we perform our part of the work during the span of physical life, will affect the conditions under which we continue our lives beyond that span. Were it otherwise, it would be the first exception of Nature's universal and fundamental law.

It therefore behooves us to study this life in ourselves and others and in all of Nature with which we come into contact here, with minute care, that we may make no more mistakes than we can help, in carrying out our obligations under the law.

Our attitude should be one of respect for all life, but not of mawkish sentimentality for it. Life itself is eternal. But Selfized Life is eternal only as we make it so. Our respect for life, therefore, should be directed chiefly toward all efforts to build up Self wherever we see it. To place one barrier in the way of the process deliberately, knowingly and without necessity, is destructive. To assist the process is to be a builder.

Every form that has life is brother to man. He is the Elder Brother. Some Souls have grown so great that they feel and therefore know the Unity of Nature. They know the meaning of Universal Brotherhood and are Elder Brothers to Men. To such as these our respect amounts to veneration, for they are our Teachers to show us the path they have trod.

But nothing is so destructive to their efforts as to place them on pedestals of god-ship, or erect iron-bound creeds from their teachings. Unless we take them into our daily lives as we do other human beings, regard them as brothers and treat them as such, we repel ourselves from them and become destructive agents to all they attempt to do for us. Never, therefore, look upon any man quick or "dead" as other than a brother. Ignorance alone makes of the wise man a thing apart to be held in awe, and his slightest wish obeyed as law.

Among students of such teachers a comradeship should prevail of utter frankness, for they are fellow travelers along the same path. Help should always be given freely when asked— but never pressed upon another who does not ask it. More time and energy is frittered away by well-intentioned reformers and would-be helpers of others in advising those who do not want it and often are not prepared to accept it, than would be necessary to give relief to all their circle of real suppliants.

We study that we may know and teach. Knowledge that is not used is a worthless thing. To constitute ones self a center of knowledge and wisdom without being ready at all times to give to others as they shall ask, cramps the Self. But in giving be sure that your gift is wanted, for not all that seek do so, from real desire to know, nor yet from motives that are constructive.

29

Students of the Great Work, yours is the most honorable calling in the world. You are engaged in coordinating the collective mind of humanity, as well as in making yourselves healthy corpuscles of its body, soul and spirit. Your individual part of the work is that of an atom or a cell as compared with the whole work. But remember, that so long as one single diseased cell remains in the body it is not in perfect health.

A TRIP TO THE VALLEY OF THE PINES
By A TRIANGLE OF STUDENTS

The Ann Arbor Council of Sadol has been holding regular meetings nearly every two weeks during the past several years, endeavoring in this manner to inculcate in their lives the teachings of the Great School of Natural Science as set forth in the text books of the able and gifted editor of this magazine; and it was not until the publication—"THE GREAT WORK IN AMERICA"—reached us that we realized how near we were living to one so ably assisting in the work of editing our magazine as our brother, Joseph A. Sadony.

At once we were reminded of the quotation that "a prophet is not known in his own country"; and after some discussion as to the feasability and ability of driving a car 196 miles, making a call of two or three hours and driving home again, without losing any working time during the week, it was finally settled that we would start at 5:30 Sunday morning, June 14, 1925, to visit The Valley of the Pines, and Brother Sadony. We wired and secured an appointment with Brother Joseph for 2 P. M. At 1:30 of that wonderful day we drove into the "Valley of the Pines", five miles out from the little town of Montague, Michigan, down a winding road, the last half mile of which was through a forest; then coming to the farm clearing, two-thirds of which is located on quite a bluff, the other one-third being the valley proper. As we drove down the deep, sandy, winding road across this clearing, it appeared no different from the many other sandy roads on which the writer has tavelled throughout the northern part of Michigan; but, as we approached the residential section of this apparently ordinary country place, we passed a common Michigan farm-house, a few rods beyond which appeared a swinging gate barring our further progress. A look about us soon disclosed the presence, in close proximity, of a kennel of eight or ten handsome police dogs, full grown and healthy looking—so we decided instanter that, rather than go crashing through the gate, due caution should be observed. One of our triangle alighted from the car and, on approaching the gate, his presence was observed by a personage within the enclosure. This individual approached our messenger, and soon thereafter the gate was opened and we drove into the "Valley of the Pines".

After parking our car where requested, we were immediately aware that we were in no ordinary farming community. Hedges seemed to radiate in many directions, with paths leading alongside and close to the numerous Carolina poplars of magnificent height, while underneath their shade a handsome rustic log house, filled with a rare collection of backwoods antiques and Indian relics, had recently been erected—the work of the Sadony family. We had not been there but a few moments when Mrs. Sadony, with her two sons—Joseph and Arthur—came down the grassy slope from their house, a few rods distant, and were introduced; after which moment, and for the ensuing four hours, one surprise after another followed so rapidly and pleasantly and with such great benefit to the visitors that, from the standpoint of the writer, no other four hours of his more than half a century of this physical life, can begin to compare.

The boys explained to us how they had built the log house. Then we were shown through the chemical and electrical shops of the older son, with its practically complete outfit—static machines, x-ray, etc. (which Mr. Gill had better describe)— then the kennel of dogs belonging to Mrs. Sadony; then gradually leading up the side of the hill we paused to witness the 200-apartment bird house with the monster pole swing close by. Thence we ascended a winding split-log pathway for fifty or sixty steps where we turned abruptly past the doorway of the workshop of Brother Joseph, and continued up the winding way, which in another fifty or sixty steps brought us to the out-door astronomical observatory, from the top of which Lake Michigan is clearly visible in clear weather.

It is now two o'clock and as we again approach the doorway of Brother Joseph's workshop, we awaken to the fact that our escort has vanished, save for the older boy, Joseph, who knocks on the door. This is opened by his father who at once greets us so cordially, and keeps this cordiality radiating so continuously throughout the visit that somehow we are assured that we are in the presence of one of our own family. No question could we ask but that an answer was ready and loaded with truths so plain that it was within our comprehension to absorb and utilize this knowledge thenceforward, and the cheerfulness and eagerness of Brother Joseph to aid us, which he did during the following three and one-half hours, and then insisting that we stay to dinner, caused us to believe that we had been in the presence of a real Master.

To show his faculty for fun, we might mention the fact that a neighbor was visiting him one day in apple time, and they were out admiring the fruit. Brother Joseph reached up and picked a particularly nice, shiny coated one, and handed it to the man who appeared quite eager for it until he discovered Mr. Sadony's picture right in the skin of the apple. He quickly handed the apple back and, quite concerned, departed abruptly, without waiting for Brother Joseph to explain how he had fastened a film of his picture on the apple and the sunlight did the rest.

At the dinner table the two boys said grace in unison—as Brother Joseph seemed to think he might forget some of it—and besides swallowing a fifty-cent piece, extracting it from the back of his neck, then immediately pulling off the end of his left thumb—all of which nonsense was followed by some truths which would imbed themselves in our consciousness—he kept interest keen to the very last farewell.

We are all agreed that it was worth many times over the trip we took, as we again returned to Ann Arbor at ten minutes after 12, Sunday, midnight. We earnestly long for more of the teachings of Brother Joseph and his wise counsellings. He

32

justifies all that our Elder Brother has told us of him in the first issue of our magazine.

Fraternally,

ALONZO D. PARKER.

Dear Friends:

We journeyed nearly 200 miles to see Brother Joseph Sadony, his family and friends, and the "bit of heaven" where they dwell. That is precisely the impression left on us three brothers and fellow-students.

It was shortly after noon when we found the eighty acres on the shore of Lake Michigan, about five miles from the little town of Montague. Leaving the main traveled road, and winding through a stretch of woods—thence on through the sandy soil toward the tall pines—we found there in a valley of these beautiful trees nestled together, the dwelling places, rustic lodge, workshop, flowers, green lawns, bird houses and all else that compose the aids to life for Brother Sadony and his family. There we were met by a cordial young man—Meredith Beyers—who welcomed us in that sincere fashion which only the heart can understand.

Mrs. Sadony and her two charming boys—one cannot help loving these boys after a trip through the fairyland of their workshop, dog kennels, pigeon roosts, etc.—greeted us with cordial hospitality. To one mechanically inclined, there is wonder upon wonder in the chemical and electrical laboratories where these boys, under their father's guidance, have come to know much of the natural laws of physical nature.

The whole assemblage of houses, shops, office, etc.—including electric light, power system, water pressure system, etc.—was built by this family with their own hands. There was every indication of love and good will for all mankind ruling supreme here.

We were invited into our friend's office, where Brother Sadony greeted us and made us feel at home. Here is where this gracious man spends many hours—often late into the night —in sending messages of hope, inspiration and helpful advice to those who need a helping Christian hand.

33

One is impressed with the strength that must come to one who gives to all who need, in the unselfish spirit evidenced by Brother Sadony. He inspires tender love, yet has the physique of a master of physical culture. He lives among the birds in the tall pines, and here, through an established harmonic relation with progressive life, he is able to tune in with the harmonies and the knowledge of the great plan of life—even to the detailed plans by the Greater Architect for the individual life—thus seeming to demonstrate a capacity which we all may acquire. The harvest is bountiful and it is written of the Master, Jesus, that he said: "All these things ye can do, and even greater things".

It is for us to witness this handiwork and, through unselfish effort and service, to prepare ourselves for a higher and higher place of service, responsibility and happiness.

Brother Sadony, his charming wife and coworker, his boys and his helpers at The Valley all offer living examples and inspirations to better lives.

Cordially,

IRVING L. GILL.

"AND I WENT ALONG"

My part in the trip to "The Valley of the Pines" came about as most successful things come to me; the first stage of which is usually accomplished with hesitancy and reluctance. A week or so before the trip Mr. Parker asked me whether or not I would like to go over and see Joseph Sadony; never having much of a curiosity, nor prone to seek out men because of something noteworthy being said about them, I said I wouldn't go very far to see any man. This was like a dash of cold water to Mr. Parker; but I had in mind the following which I once heard a United States Senator say: "I always supposed the United States Senate was composed of great men until I became one myself, then I changed my mind."

But undaunted in purpose, Mr. Parker approached Mr. Gill on the subject at our next Council meeting, and after the boys had planned the trip I told them that "I'd go along". So we made the journey without incident; even the Speed Cop in some way missed us and we arrived in Montague in time for the mid-day meal. Inquiring of the hotel keeper the way to The Valley of the Pines, we secured the desired information and found our informant to be a real good-natured fellow and so took dinner at his hotel. The meal was good and the dining room appointments were cheerful and homelike; so our first point of contact with Mr. Sadony's immediate surroundings were very pleasant, to say the least.

Our meal over we took a stroll, for our appointment with Brother Joseph was not until two o'clock, so we had some time to kill. We walked to the bridge which separates Whitehall and Montague; took in the surroundings and viewed the stadium across White Lake, where the International Yacht Races were recently held. By this time it was time to get in our car and cover the last five-mile lap of our trip, which skirted White Lake, until we came to a point where fresh tar had just been put on the road; and lo! Providence had seemingly ordained that we should even escape the tar, for here was our turn onto a lane-like road which leads through the thickets and pines to Brother Sadony's place.

As Mr. Parker and Mr. Gill have taken you through the buildings and about the grounds, I shall simply add that every improvement of this little heaven, created in the midst of a northern wilderness, was accomplished by Mr. Sadony and his family during the eighteen years which they have lived there. It was here that the boys "Joseph" and "Arthur" were born, and the harmonic relation existing in this little family is self-evident from the fact that Mr. and Mrs. Sadony have not been separated one complete day in all that eighteen years. With their own hands this little family beautified the grounds and erected the buildings that grace them. Mr. Sadony, with his own hands, made the machine for making the cement blocks; made the blocks and laid them into the buildings; and Mrs. Sadony proudly declares, "and I helped, too".

Mr. Sadony's office and study is an unpretentious little

building situated on the side of a hill some distance from the other buildings and overlooks the beautiful lawns and gardens, with their paths and rustic seats which stretch out below. Here he whom we three had come to affectionately call "Brother Joseph" greeted us with a warmth of handclasp and glow of friendly greeting radiating from his kindly face, seldom equaled, and, we believe, never excelled in genuine sincerity.

Here in this combination office, study and library, we found ourselves surrounded by thousands of books, both ancient and modern, and gathered from every quarter of the globe. Aside from books there were relics and antiques of every conceivable description, some of great antiquity. They have been *given* to Brother Sadony by those whom he has *befriended,* and have been sent by people of every nationality and from every part of the earth. As Mr. Sadony will not accept pay for his services, these things have been given him as tokens of appreciation by the thousands whom he has befriended and helped.

Quite naturally, I presume, our readers will say, "You have told us considerable about The Valley of the Pines, but you haven't told us much as to your impressions of Mr. Sadony". Well, in a sense, perhaps, that is true; but to tell you in such a way as to give a true word picture and yet not excite that seeming innate tendency of human nature to *idolize* is perhaps difficult to do. In the first place, Mr. Sadony is just a plain red-blooded man. However, we believe he is a true Prophet of the Great White School. And we want to say to you, don't try to fool him; you can't.

The three of us rather believe that we were fully awake and in possession of our right senses; if so, there is no question as to the ability of Mr. Sadony to measure up to any claims made by our Elder Brother concerning his power to prophesy. All three of us are very familiar with the prattle of the fortune teller and Test Medium; and to one who is at all schooled in the Constructive and Destructive Principle of Nature in relation to psychic phenomena, it is not at all difficult to distinguish between the sane and sensible tests and predictions of this Independent Psychic and that of Mediumship.

The difference is exactly parallel with the person who sees a thing himself and tells about it, and one who tries to tell what someone else shows him or compels him to recite. The former is clear cut and has the evidence of Truth and dependability; the latter of confusion and uncertainty, to say the least. The Independent Psychic will differentiate between that which is Constructive and that which is Destructive and determine that which is best to tell and that which is proper to keep to himself; that is because the Independent Psychic is in possession of his Rational Powers; and this is exactly what Mr. Sadony does.

Very few words passed between Mr. Sadony and myself during the four hours we men were assembled; for I was there to take advantage of all the information I could get, and it kept me busy listening. However, within a few days after reaching home I received a four-page letter, of commercial letter size and closely written, in answer to many of the thoughts which went through my mind at the time we were with him; so you see it was all right for me to save my breath.

If one expects to find in Mr. Sadony a display of pretentiousness and show, one is destined to disappointment; for Brother Joseph is just a plain, unpretentious man and gentleman; and one who can wear the cloth or don the overalls with equal facility and with full approval of conscience. The wealthy and the poor, if they are conscientious, are equal in his sight. The fact that Mr. Sadony and his family have cleared, improved and beautified the land and have built the buildings which they occupy, with their own hands, would seem to indicate that the fundamental principle at the basis of his conception of things is that one should, in so far as possible, create that which one uses and enjoys.

After spending several hours in Brother Joseph's study we were conducted to the home, where we spent a delightful hour and partook of a splendid dinner. I am sure that the unfeigned and remarkable hospitality of our host and hostess will never be forgotten by us three men; and, by the way, if you ever want a good piece of strawberry shortcake, try and get on the right side of Mrs. Sadony.

W. W. MANN.

A CREED OF ANNIHILATION
By W. T. R. MORRIS

Can it be possible that anyone in this enlightened age, who claims long since to have evolved from the animal, believes in a creed of annihilation? You certainly cannot say for the individual who looks upon a future from this dreary viewpoint, that he is a rational being; for no individual endowed with reason and the capacity of understanding, could accept such a blighting credenda. While such an individual may possess a degree of intelligence, he most assuredly cannot be said to reason.

We all love to live. This love of life animates every living thing. Man alone hopes for immortality. Every man wants to live after he has put off this mortal body—whether he admits it or not. And while there may be doubt in our minds as to the position of some men on this question, when the truth is known —when these men have been brought face to face with the question, they will say that they desire to live on after this transition called Death.

What can this physical life be if we do not possess this natural hope and expectation of a life to come? Except for this hope and expectation man could not properly work out his destiny upon this, or any other plane. If this transition, called Death, is the end, why do we on this physical plane, possess the high ideals that we have? Why give any thought to anything which is noble, exalting or altruistic? If there is no spiritual life. let us then make this physical life as materialistic a life as we can. Why should we try to improve ourselves for the future? Improve ourselves for what? For total annihilation?

Ah! We know that this life is but a school of experience to fit us for a higher life of the Soul. We have our lessons to learn; and we know that our status hereafter is conditioned by the life we live here. Our activities on this physical plane either carry us forward, or drag us down.

Faith is a perpetual inspiration; skepticism clouds the best efforts. A creed of annihilation dries up the secret springs of human knowledge. It clouds the finest ambitions, and thwarts the finest possibilities.

How sickening to the Soul to think that Nature's greatest handiwork—Man—must go down to total annihilation, after he has lived nobly on this physical plane.

No! It cannot be. Man has breathed into his nostrils the Soul Element—the Breath of Life—and even as ignorant as he may be, as coarse and as savage as he may be, the expectation of a future life—something beyond the grave—comes to him as an intuition, later dawning into hope and then springing triumphantly up into a rational Faith. And, at last, we know that he who has both Faith and Hope may acquire Actual Knowledge.

Then why should men cling to a creed of annihilation, knowing that actual knowledge of a life to come would fix and ennoble life's purpose as no fitful hope nor wavering faith can ever do? Is it not reasonable to suppose if he does so, it is because he has yet to know the Law? Why *believe* a thing when you can *know* it? The doctrine of Jesus Christ testifies to a personal and exact knowledge of the spiritual side of life. He proved the Law. It was a personal experience to him when he demonstrated the Law. He proved the Law by "living the life".

Any creed that takes away from the individual man or woman that expectation of a life beyond, which arises out of conditions which distinctly are not physical, is born of the blackness of night, and not of the light of the Soul.

When the truth is discovered, we find that all of life's duties, when constructively performed, are done in order that the individual may be better prepared to face the future. A man without hope or desire, merely exists; he can scarcely be said to live.

Again, if this actual knowledge of a spiritual side of life can be had, why not seek it? Why accept something else? Why still cling to a belief, when you can *know* the truth? Why hold on to hope, faith or even belief, when actual knowledge is at hand, provided you have the Intelligence, the Courage and the Perseverance to prove the Law? Actual knowledge can be had. It can be had by a personal experience.

This personal experience which the lowly Nazarene had leaves no room for a creed of annihilation, but substitutes the Law of Life, and proves that you, yourself, can "prove the Law"—can come into possession of the exact knowledge, if you will but "Live the Life".

UNITY

By ABBIE GERRISH-JONES

The lovely flower, the bird, the bee,
The sunshine and the spreading tree,
In God's own Light expand and grow;
One life, One love, One Father know.

So must we give our loving care
To God's dear creatures, everywhere.
Because we know that they and we
Belong to one big family.

Since God is Life, then He must be
In every shrub and flower and tree.
In bird and beast, in wind and rain,
In sun and stars, in hill and plain.

Then must each child, both great and small,
Of the Dear Father of us all,
Love all these other children, too;
God gives them life, as He does you.

Harmonic Literature

THE HARMONIC SERIES

Vol. 1. **Harmonics of Evolution,** by Florence Huntley, **$3.00**

Vol. II. **The Great Psychological Crime** -   -   **$3.00**

Vol. III. **The Great Work**   -   -   -   **$3.00**

Vol. IV. **The Great Known** by J. E. Richardson, **(TK)** **$3.00**

The Higher Aspect of Nursing, by Noneta S. Richardson, **$2.00**

(Applies the Principles of the Great School to LIFE)

THE HARMONIC BOOKLET SERIES

(Each booklet contains the practical application of a vital Principle to the LIVING OF THE LIFE.

One subscription for entire series of 12 Booklets

$3.00

Single copies, 25c each. 5 copies of **Same Booklet,** $1.00

Back numbers can be had on order   -   - 25c

Special reductions for large lots, **of any one booklet.**

THIS MAGAZINE

One Subscription for one year   -   - $ 3.50

Ten Subscriptions for one year   -   - $30.00

Address all orders with remittance, to

J. E. RICHARDSON

8186 Marmont Lane

Hollywood, California

CPSIA information can be obtained
at www.ICGtesting.com
Printed in the USA
BVHW041716030119
536774BV00057B/834/P